The Ride of Yeldis

& Other Poems

Francis Vielé-Griffin

Translated By Richard Robinson

Sunny Lou Publishing Company
Portland, Oregon, USA
http://www.sunnyloupublishing.com

Original Publication Date: 2023 June 25

ISBN: 978-1-955392-39-6

# # #

This translation from French is based on the
Léon Vanier, Libraire-Éditeur edition of *Le
chevauchée d'Yeldis et autres poèmes*, Paris,
1893.

Contents

Foreword

From chapter one, book one, of *Francis Vielé-Griffin: His Work, His Thought, His Art*, by Jean de Cours, published by the Librairie Ancienne Honoré Champion, Paris, 1930.

THE RIDE OF YELDIS

The Ride of Yeldis, which appeared in 1893, is said to be the synthesis of the preceding collections.[1] It embodies the same thought. But through the graces that legend always possesses, we discover a finesse in the psychology that had hardly found the opportunity to come to light. As in all the dramatic or legendary poems by F. Vielé-Griffin, the subject is marvelously simple and holds value primarily through the meaning that results, and through the art by which it is developed. Five young men fall in love with Yeldis. Although the poem opens with "an image, an evocation" that seemed to M. Charles Maurras "so beautiful one wants to shout" –

> *The turrets that covered Her with their*
> *shadow*
> *Rose like organ pipes against the sky,*

I myself am more struck by certain character traits like the one in which the poet notes, among one of the

---

[1] The preceding collections: which include *Cull of April*, *Swans*, *Joys*, all three of which are published by Sunny Lou Publishing.

young men, Philarque, the beginnings of a love:

> *And we saw Yeldis among the flowers;*
> *Philarque, counting the old gold ducats,*
> *Thought he recognized her in the effigies*
> *And had to count over, and messed up again...*

But Yeldis' father passes away, and Yeldis announces to her five suitors that she is leaving on a journey:

> *However*
> *Yeldis with her train of sorrowful darkness*
> *Came, in the rustling sound of the gravel*
>   *under her feet,*
> *Paler with her long eyes of amethyst*
> *And her hair rose-colored and scaffolded;*
> *Violet gloved, she...*

     * * *

> *"The journey is distant," she said,*
> *"From the edge of dawn,*
> *And I go alone, without a knight even,*
> *Without a squire who rides in the saddle!"*
> *She laughed, as if to mock us,*
> *Knowing that each of us would follow her,*
> *League after league, step after step,*
> *Through false path and true path,*
> *Until trespass.*

And the ride begins; they go through towns and fields, but:

> *One radiant day,*

Philarque and Luc both quit the path
And rode off, without saying goodbye,
Towards the Western sun,
As if in flight;
Yeldis smiled and whipped her horse;
Martial and Claude turned away, pale;
And we followed her, the three of us, without
saying a word.

On another day, Claude dies in his sleep, and, on yet another day, Martial declares his love to Yeldis.

He took her and, without a cry and without
resistance,
Without a word spoken between them,
Jumped into the stirrups,
And giddyap! the horse reared and went into
a gallop...

He was beautiful in his full youth,
She blushed for all his promises;
Doubtless, their fates were bound.

And the poet, left alone, tells us his thought:

I am not ashamed of myself, thinking on it,
I have not the least regret for this poem:
I know that, for having followed Her
Under the chestnut trees, I now know life:

* * *

Not a moment to ask forgiveness for;

With a single smile She made me thus;
If I had not been born for her kiss,
At the very least, I gave her my soul – She left
The secret of her soul to this heart of mine:

* * *

There is not a blade of grass that quivers,
There is not a pebble that rolls in the river,
Not a song in the autumn orchard,
Not a kiss on the spring path,
Not a drop of true blood in the West,
Not a sacred word vibrating in Poems,
That I do not weep over or laugh over, that I
*   do not love in Her.*

The three last lines of the *envoi* give the poem
its meaning:

And, bent over the sheaf that was gleaned for
*   you,*
I listen to the bells ringing in the evening,
And I think that Life is beautiful and full of
*   Hope.*

A beautiful, sensible, and profound conclusion
to a poem that Charles Maurras considered "of so in-
decisive and pale a beauty, so traversed here and there
with sudden, blinding lights, such gorgeous and ten-
der pages, as to be read and reread and meditated on.
I do not know what holds me back from hailing M. F.
Vielé-Griffin here as a master." Such is, it seems to
me, the impression that French men of letters must
have felt when the poet collected in 1895 all the po-

ems of his youth, which I have laboriously endeavored to analyze, in a single and important volume, entitled *Poèmes et Poésies*.

Preface

Preface

To the reader,

Leave aside, for one moment, the daily concerns that afflict you; leave aside as well the esthetics that alternately extolled *realism* and *idealism*; believe that there has never been an antagonism between Reality and the Ideal, but that it is from their fusion that Life is forged; forget also the skilled metricists – wind passes through the poplars – and accept, simply, as I offer it to you, this little bit of me.

If your dream resonates here, at times, in unison with my words, my effort will not have been in vain – otherwise, forget even to blame me, and go your way without rancor.

– F. V.-G.

Laundresses

Laundresses

The air vibrates here along the pink shores' edge
And rises towards the bright broom;
There is nothing holier
In this sweet, glorious mystery
Than your gestures, laundresses.

Among the poplars reflected
In the great Loire tributary
Is the linen that a skillful hand extends,
Unfolds, floats, clear and vague,
Processes subtly, and turns over,
And stretches in the current like an algae.

And their songs pass over the Marne
Undoubtedly;
To the lapping sound of young mangles
That, tired, drip,
The merry sounds of young women's voices
Intersect, join,
And in the refrains that grow distant
I hear the merry song of the battledores
Giving rhythm to the immemorial hours.

The sorrow! If the immensity of life
Is not contained entirely in one hour, such that
One word of love equals the flickering
Light of the emotional star of childhood evenings;
Sorrow! If the only word respoken
Is not the word of Paradise,

If all things are not the same.
And if there are new poems...

Old Hellas, heroic mother
Of a millennium-old youthful dream,
Works the scythe in the thyme, all her beautiful
          warlike life,
Sun drenched, blinding under the metal,
And passes in theories towards victory,
Stirring the dust that falls onto gray laurels
          blossoming in glories,
Massacring her beauty on Trojan battlefields
Where Helen, the pain of all joy, –
Burning her beautiful life of love that alone
          dominates
At the altars of Paphos and Amathonte,
Rises from another bloody shore...
The old woman Hellas is dead – she lives! I see
The royal laundress with the rosy arms, –
A Nausicaa of modest pose
Who is moved solely by innocent pity,
And smiles, not afraid of a naked Ulysses.

Old Rome,
Strong,
Haughty, and sad,
Vain, and with no art but for hegemony,
You who trampled with heavy foot the Ionian orchard
And made the true blood of Christ infecund.
With your laws, your legions,
Mother of formularies,
You brutalized nations
And over your stone highways,

Sterile and loveless Rome,
You led the emperor by a short sword,
In a word, Rome...
Your yoke is heavy.

Life, certainly, is vile this evening, but beautiful still:
I do not know if, outside of itself, it holds any hope:
But hope merits faith, and faith begets love;
Night, which lies and groans, is pregnant with a new
            dawn;
Vile Life, certainly, is beautiful still this evening
And faith embraces us as our turn approaches.

At twilight, then, you whom the task holds back.
Laundress with the rosy arms, o young woman,
Smiling, redeem the hatred in our souls,
The ultimate desire for life is in your care;
Tell us – for having seen it – smiling in your tears.
The ever-new water reflecting the same flowers,
The slow rise of the poplars toward heaven,
The road,
Open forever toward similar doubts,
The road where young knights go;
Tell us that everything in life is beautiful and
            worth living for,
That all those old poems in new books
Are written in harmony with your voice along the
            espaliers,
In accordance with your song in the orchards where
            God flourishes,
And tell us that love hopes, and believes, and wants.

And you, sad Forebear, with the thin arm, with the
        slow gesture,
Who wash, kneeling, late into the evening,
Remind us of the eternal promise
In your monotonous and quiet song:
Night falls, the mystery fades
Behind the veil of a past of rust and carnage,
Make it pure, august Forebear of ancient times,
Like a sheer bridal veil,
And, rising up, solemn, in the morning breeze,
Hold out toward the East the dawn of white linen.

The Gravedigger

The Gravedigger

The old rampart in the August sun;
All the air vibrating at the ruddy crest
Of the low wall that runs along the path;
The old rampart in the August sun,
White and ivyless – hoary almost –
At the flowering foot of the nettle, or bare;
The old ancient wall,
White, and with no shadow but mine.

Under this sun and in this grass,
I heard Life whispering
As if in the stubble around the sheaves
On every stone a grey, motionless
Lizard that someone could have reached out
With his hand, and taken.

In a forced smile of farewell,
Reseen in a smile of greeting:
Like *my* old age come peacefully,
With none of the fuss of mourning,
Smiling seriously at my twenty years
Standing against the old white wall.

For, even though this great and serious old man
Was deaf and did not speak,
Conscious decision by those who know,
(In a broad, sweeping gesture, with the heavy
Forged-iron key that he held,
Mowing down the horizon, peak after peak),

I heard him, rhyme after rhyme,
My eyes half-closed, my heart far away:

"I do not know who is more pitiful:
He who comes out to meet Life
Or he who turns away from it;
I do not know what is more fearful,
Young hope extinguished
Or the memory that lingers
Deep in the heart, forever,
Like a stone dropped into a lake:
But I believe I know now
That there were no such divisions
Between our fictitious years,
That there is no old age:
One soul is old at dawn,
Another is still young at evening.

"I know that the suffering of living
Is to dream of dying
And to walk since morning
(Like someone who dreamed he was being followed)
Turning one's head around at every turn
To see what will not be seen again.

"Look: I have lived seventy years
In these very places where I was born
And if I had not seen my son grow older
And his son grow taller,
I would not have felt any older
Than the evening we returned home together:
I am standing in the sun
As if twenty years old, too;
And I feel younger than you...

There is one thing in my heart, however,
That accumulates over time
(Like sand falling grain by grain
That bars the way one morning,
Grain by grain like the dune does),
One grows wise in spite of oneself:
I know the sky, the wind, the moon,
I know the remedies one chooses
And when the hour of rest arrives,
When one must lie down in the coffin
And when Death comes with intention..."

Thus did I dream in the bright sun,
Eyes half-closed and, in a half state
Of visionary wakefulness, full of dreams
Speaking deceitful words perhaps,
Or words of wisdom even,
To the mute, slow, and serious old man
– Hand on his forehead, against the door,
Leaning, under the keystone,
With a far-off gaze at the bright waves...
He could have been taken for stone.

He opened the clock tower before me;
Its silver face and his shovel, polished
By the maternal earth,
Gleamed in the half-light, in a cross shape;
The weights of the clock hung low,
And the pendulum swung back and forth
For seventy years:
Counting the days – his, mine;
It had lived because of his life

For, every day, he came
With the large key he held in hand
To wind the chain, turn after turn.
So that it might live one more day
And so time might not die...

That moment cannot die;
It is inside me, young and serene
With my twenty years, of which it is queen:
It is inside me, like Hope,
Like Thought and its joy,
Like yours, alive this evening,
Wise in your twenty young years,
Like its wisdom surprised
By the radiant mystery of being –
Such that in it, I may be reborn.

Diptych

Diptych

(To be painted)

Over here is a plain of tall red wheat
That a monk from Fiésole dreamed of;[2]
Look at the scythe seen gleaming:
The scythe is beautiful
That flies
Swiftly
Like a black wing in the red wheat;
Death is beautiful and silent,
And cuts and cuts in large swaths,
And its harvest is good and beautiful.

With his sickle,
Comely Love culls flowers
From among the stubble,
Culls and weeps
And sings
And walks alone
Without fright;
And Death walks before Him
With its scythe that gleams and gleams
– Draped in the shroud of dawn,
It mows speechlessly and silently
Millions of tall ears of wheat.

---

[2]A monk from Fiésole: Fra Angelico (AD 1395-1455), a Dominican friar and Early Italian Renaissance painter.

There it is, on the gold panel;
It pushes the Autumn plow:
The long field unfolds in furrows
Carting the pale and dead stubble;
And behind It, He continues
With more golden ears
In his adolescent hair,
With always the same song
And always sowing, in old furrows,
In the golden light of a paling sun, –
He sows hearts by the millions.

Do you care to weep while he sings?
To love is to die and be reborn;
What poor delusion frightens you?
Are you afraid of knowing yourself?
Look again and live your life
According to a vision of joy:
Love's sickle diverts,
The scythe spreads like a wing;
Look: Love cuts with its wing
The tallest lilies while the willows weep,
Death stops and his black scythe
Is like a wing,
Like a wing at his shoulder!

Rejoice, and learn to believe.

Flowers of
the Path

Flowers of the Path

In an odor of tossed hay,
In a murmur of the rustic ford,
Through the diaphanous shade,
Come: oblique shadow,
The hay smells of love,
The water's song is tender, silent, grave
Like a distant canticle
– The year has made its round.

All the sheepfolds are the same
And in my verses some sheep will come –
Like this evening, towards Indre – gathered in a
        ring,
To bleat the simplest of poems –
That we will laugh over;
It is not until the unforeseen storm
That facilitates heroism (do recall),
And I will be so brave under lightning flashes
(And, my faith! you have seen me do as much)
That I will merit your proud kisses;
Come, June has flowered the meadows and the woods
And the tomorrows are yesterdays
… I think?…

A bridge spans the river
Bounding from isle to isle
Between willow trees and poplars;
Let us cross; every song resonates under the arches
The blue hour is new
When beside me you march,
I have kisses by the thousand,
And by the thousands.

Will we visit the vineyards in blossom,
Will we go through the meadow grass,
Or under the shade of young ash trees,
Will we go beyond the purple-tinged sunsets?
– Every road is distant.

At the beautiful hour, – we must separate,
You adorned of dreams and roses,
Towards vaguenesses and a night that is forever lost...

I waited for you like a lover however,
I made my soul dream of your return even,
I made my chastity from your naked shoulder
Shivering from my kiss in anticipation;

From far away, when I raised my eyes, from far
        away,
It was you who was tossing the fresh hay,
It was you who was gathering the new grape,
And it was your step, a total fluttering of wings;

You were my hope, and here you are come again,
Laughing and fragile in your naked beauty.
Pregnant with joy and love, and who were...
Between yesterday and tomorrow there is no
        today,
And I have never – on my soul! – known you.

Days of mourning when you depart
Like black swans to crepuscular lakes,
The barque is empty that you pull;
I will go to the end of unrivaled dreams,
I will go to the east of bright candors
Where one's unsheathed illusions are brandished!

Up to the road, arduous for those who lack faith,
The forest is dying in the scrubs; –
Road of blue lands where the most worthy is king,
Predestined road
That runs, radiant like a year,
Through a plain of reprisals!...

From there, where the dawn breaks,
Born like a tear from a sob,
It flows forever, wave upon wave,
Toward the day that dies and the night that weeps,
The river that does not rest for more than one hour...

Dream of Eden with clear fountains,
Dreams of long embalmed gardens,
Alms offered to all our prayers
So that our hearts might be loved:

Behold our feast day, dead only yesterday,
The Lamb of the offering, we have immolated it,
The wave is far that we watched intently,
The florid river has flowed away.

A flower has died this summer evening;
My heart is disconsolate.

Imperturbed rivers of love
Where I have washed away the carnage of living;
Luminous heavens whose splendor releases;
Oceans of sweetness bending into the distances
Toward lands whose vague names intoxicate...

Ever *forward*! The road is traveled
By small desires and craven prides;
My soul is strong and was succored
By joyful kisses and mournful tears...
Look, just above the hill, the star that appeared...

The Bear and
the Abbess

The Bear and the Abbess

"... and since then that animal refused to abandon her, but remained among the wise virgins, not like a furious bear, but gentler than a lamb."

– Life of Saint Goule

Except for the wind's laughter in the beech trees
And the fallen beechmast
In rusty leaves;
Except, perhaps,
For the distant horn that weeps its pain,
The silence is so great, on porch and threshold,
That one hears through the gate,
Open to the holy woods that contemplate,
The quiet prayer of white nuns
Preparing for the Sunday vigil.
Through the gate, with its heavy, solid arch,
The invited forest
Exhales its incense at the radiant altar
Where all flowers from its mouth
Kiss the Crucified's bleeding feet;
The wind utters a stammered prayer...
The forest wafts through the gate, to God,
To the monstrance at the Crucified's feet,
And to his fiery wounds that bleed
In holy pity on the universe;

Disturbing this peaceful adoration,
A hunting party noisily hurtles through the valley:
And the pack of dogs is frenzied

In the dark shadows.
And the deep-sounding horn
Bellows through the coppices,
So that the pale and frail abbess,
Facing the open gate,
Looks and sees in the bright background
A bear on the threshold; he approaches
And lies down, submissive at her feet;
And the nuns pray, focusing on their souls
While, seen inside the same stone frame,
The howling pack runs through the glade
Under the servants' whip, who block its escape;
And the Emperor dismounts who
Crosses himself and devoutly enters.

The abbess rises then and says:
"Charlemagne, sanctuary is inviolable."
And the Emperor kneels and prays
Before resuming his hunt through the valley.

That season comes when days begin to shorten.
The bear followed the abbess in the cloister
Where nuns go and come, praying to the Lord;
And, lying outside her cellule door, he sleeps,
Only to follow her again, on waking, through the
            corridor,
To Matins, Lauds, the holy sanctum even;
And to the orchard where wool is spun,
The bear followed her like a page the queen.

Except for Prayer, when one speaks to God,
No words were spoken in that tranquil place,

And the bear, thus, understood the abbess
Who spoke with a glance or a caress;
And in silence, the abbess knew
How to read what they dreamt, the bear's eyes;
Thus did they speak, of things one is ignorant of,
For words are too sonorous,
Life is brutal and banal in itself,
And silence is an eternal tongue
Wherein lofty and sacred things
Float from dream to dream, thought to thought,
And an ample idea is exchanged without
        dissimulation
Of poor words from brazen lips:
A friendly silence wherein the Beauty and Beast
Speak the poet's language.

The pale and frail abbess spoke words to him
Too, stroking his neck with a steady hand,
And relived her dream of ancient concern:
"Good bear, your life and mine are similar
And this is why we love each other:
I too lived in calm woods,
In my father's green donjon, friend:
No sound of war stirred violent emotion then,
No night transpired when I could not sleep,
Calm beside my mother;
You, you lived in the blue forest,
Tell me, good bear, were you content?"
And in his upturned eyes of a dark hue
She could read the tranquil dream of the forest.

"Once there came a lord who found me beautiful,

Offered his hand, but I rebuffed him;
And my father had to raise the drawbridge,
Unwilling to surrender me;
His assault was terrible, I shudder to this day!
Good bear! do you remember the horn?..."
And she read in his upturned eyes
The nocturnal terror of the forest.

"Vanquished, my father gave me over,
And I prayed to God for help:
I put on the black veil and white robe
And, running from love and its vileness,
Like you, I came to the foot of the altar
Where, on a Sunday eve, I found sanctuary;
So that on the vigil of the Lord's day,
The gate stands wide open to the glade –
An invitation to hospitable prayer
For all those seeking God and sanctuary;
And this is how we two are
Chosen for silence and prayer, good bear,"
She said, and she saw that his golden eyes
Prayed the prayer of the forest.

"My life draws to a close, now; I would like
That heaven's gate open its door to me:
And that you pass over the sill with me,
Just like the day you came in from the forest;
Heaven would be bleak without your bright eye
Following me, constantly, speaking to me, watching
       over me:
I would like to go, with you, to God."
– She bowed her head and kissed his ear.

She sat under a flowering tree
That was dropping pale tears onto her lap,
The June sun cast a golden light
Over the cloister steps;
The wagtail's song was scarcely sonorous;
Head on his shoulder, she dreamed perhaps.
For, on opening her eyes in the bright sun,
Where the beautiful bear should have been
She saw JESUS, in all his vermillion glory,
Who said, with an indefinite smile,
As one might smile at a child's prattle:
"My frail and pale little abbess,
Your little soul be blessed,
For the pity of your virginal heart;
Come, my father grants your request:
It was Me, your God, the impoverished animal."

Saint Martinian

Saint Martinian

She was queen then, of Caesarea,
By the beauty adorned her of God,
And by the craven love that makes us
Sots always, and fools sometimes.
He, tired of all this and that,
Gifted his gold to the Poor and ran off
Until, by the misery of his imprudent heart,
He died in solitude, pious.

Despite the vain remorse he caused us,
His strong will was a recomfort to all,
And, although we were cowardly, we praised his
          manly mourning
And we were proud of his fierceness somewhat:
For that bitter shame of loving her
On account of her perfumed smile,
On account of her haughty look and slender hands
And her bright red-painted nails
And the voluptuousness of her disdain –
Made our young girls so vain
So that only the noble nature of the good Martinian,
Of gentle voice, remained,
Who had scorned her on all our behalf.

We praised him, but she laughed at us:
"The road is there, why not take it?"
We stood silent and took her contempt,
Content to listen to her at that price even.
Then she said: "Fine courage that!

His contempt for my beauty!
Was I not someone whom people
Kneel down before, on seeing my power?
Did he run, the poor man, for my beauty?
His great courage is cowardice."

We remained silent, not knowing how to reply;
She defied us to confound her
And said suddenly (I think she loved him):
"If I followed him into the woods,
The mere rustle of my robes in the grass –
He would shudder for love, his proud heart;
And my kiss, – 'Fie on it!' he would say, –
He would trample on his Crucifix!"

We were revolted by those words:
"'Zoe,' I said to her, "despite all the roles
That your cursed beauty plays
And though it please you to scorn
The tears of wives and mothers,
Never under heaven or on earth was there
A more vile dream than this dream of yours;
Go away, we defy you!" – She went away.

Night
(I learned about these things much later),
Night fell from heaven and calmed the cypresses;
Rain in heavy drops on the road
Made it seem like walking in a hallucination;
So much so that to the sudden sounds and shrill voice
That calls him,
Martinian, kneeling in the darkness –

His heart beating for countless seconds –
Felt death graze him with its wing,
Was afraid, cried like a sailor whose ship was
        sinking:
"Your voice! What does she want from me?
Satan, you who wander in the tenebrae" –
And he resumed loudly his doleful psalms.

"I've walked since dawn, it's raining, I'm cold;
Sanctuary, in the name of the Lord who died on the
        cross!"
He wished to say: "Shake off the dust!"
But, thinking on the merits of the Good Samaritan,
Where it is said: Knock and the door will open,
He made the sign of the cross and,
Calmly, opened the door and made fire,
So the old woman who knocked in God's name
Might dry her clothes, and rest her bones;
Then, turning to the cross where his Christ bled
He picked up his seven sad psalms again.

She spoke – garrulous like old women,
Sometimes in a half voice, sometimes as they say
In a shrill and raucous voice, – like the wind
That whispers, falls silent, sleeps, then wakes up
        again, suddenly,
And babbles nonsense in your ear –

He was praying – "God, spare me your fury,
And judge me not in anger."
She spoke – "It grew dark before the hour.
I lost my way in the clearing..."

He prayed, while the interminable babbling
Of the old woman filled his ears
To the degree that, taken by lassitude, he understood,
Against his will, the words' meaning.

First it was "Caesarea...", then other indistinct words:
He heard the voluptuous sound of the waves...
She said, "The night..." and it was, in spite of himself,
Like moonlight shining on the City...
"... The doors were closed..." – he thought of the door
He had loudly slammed;
And his shame was so great that in his troubled soul
His prayer, frantically, made him tremble,
And covering his ears with his hands
He began to chant what he tried so hard to pray.

When he took a breath between long versets,
The Voice was so loud and clear in hurried phrases,
That it seeped into his heart in iridescent drops
Like an inebriating poison that *She* had poured,
Again! like before, on those Caesarean evenings...

At that moment, turning round, he saw the blinding
And mad vision of his damnation:

Zoe appeared, standing out in the shadows,
Her ivory and pink flesh in the glow of the hearth,
With her hair flowing,
Like the Cytherean,
Pink as the dawn, emerging from the waves –
Silent and radiating, so much so that he wept;

He took a step, then fell to his knees,
Shielding his eyes with one arm while
The other waved her away with a disgusted gesture:
But she kissed his outstretched hand.

Then, turning to her, he slowly said:
"In terms of the flesh, I still love you, desperately,
For all flesh is vile and God suffers similarly,
But I love you, Zoe, also, for your soul,

"And I want you so pure and chaste and beautiful
That God might make wings of your blonde hair,
And your sweet voice project harmoniously
Before the golden throne of a blessed Life..."

He spoke slowly, and with a very calm gesture
He extended his right hand into the fire
And burned it, while admonishing her in a calm voice
For all her vain concern, and for the sins of the flesh.

"I love you," he said, "while my body cries mercy,
According to the one love of Him here,
Who let all his sweet blood, for your sins..."
Taking a bleeding crucifix in his unharmed hand,
He said: "Come with a kiss to purify your mouth,
These wounds will purify the shame of your lips."
Zoe, trembling – still draped in the purple veil
That was wont to hide her shame and depravity –
In a timid kiss that heaven still marvels at,
Drank from God's wounds the Wine that no human
Arbor ripens for human drunkenness,
And that makes one stagger towards heaven,
The wine of which it was said, in the New Testament:
"Take and drink all of you, for This is my Blood."

She went off to die near Bethlehem
Where He was born whom the Magdalene loved;
Martinian died, and I have told his story.
Jesus, crucified, sees human suffering:
Is it for the sins of the world, too, that one loves?

Epitaph

Epitaph

... I have wanted to die for a long time now. – Letter
from a twelve-year-old suicide, *Journals*, d. 1891

*... Go, for the love of Christ, to learn in death the
dogma of the resurrection...* – Paul Adam

"You are a man!" you were often told,
And, beaming, it was your youthful pride;
And better for you not to have been born,
And to sleep – at large – in your coffin;
Better to die as you die, I believe,
Better to turn away from our indignity.

Why lift your slender shoulders
To bear the architrave of the balcony of the living?
Go, die, you have seen too much:
Twenty violent emotions, joyful or morose,
Fail in your heart and are denied;
One waits for your flesh because it is rare
(No more births now, death has one leg up) –
One waits for your young flesh, son of hazard,
At the corner butcher's.

At least you know to choose death,
And know how to die, without foolish fear:
Cowardice, it is to work without bread,
The slow suicide of mines and furnaces;
Do not tremble, be strong
In your disdain
And strike against Life, child without bread...

The flesh you paid, proud and serene,
Like a coin burning in someone's hand –
Knew better intoxications, however,
That made, for eighteen times one hundred years,
The gasping survival of one hour
There and then, for one time only, ring:
At the Third Hour when *all was consummated*.

The sounds of the Easter carillon – whose echo,
Sorrowful still, vibrated towards you from another
            dawn –
Were sweet and solemn music
And bore testimony in April
To perpetual renewal...

I believe the things I wanted to tell you:
It falls like a ray of light on whoever meditates,
The pensive night is illuminated suddenly
By a flash of lightning that makes all darkness vain;
It chants one Word whose echo
Trembles, weakened, in stammered verse...

Reckless doubtless, conscious perhaps,
You killed yourself without blaspheming your being;
I think you are wise, and scrutinize your example, –
No wisdom can be evaded –
A blond-haired Child, long ago, amazed the Temple,
Wise among the Judean elders.

You were Life surging in the winds of hope
From Calvary to Vendémiaire, drunk on believing,
You were the Life of sonorous battles

And you bravely took your own life, long ago, again,
At the Thermopylae of all your hearths;
And when you died, beaming, *for the Fatherland*,
Your heart believed, assuredly,
And, assuredly in death even, you were Life.

For Life is beautiful and holy,
Life is joy and sorrow and mystery,
And in order to die, as you did, fearlessly,
One must love the dream of the earth:
They lied about it, those who made of it
A little mortal bread, a little mortal wine;
They killed you thrice, those who denied
Love and God and your humanity;
But they made your Life in the image of their shame;
By repulsing *their life,* you dominated them.

Assuredly, equal to the glaives and torches
Brandished on palace thresholds, under porches,
Assuredly, better than the hatred sown with Gold
That rises in revolt out of the oppressed soil,
Better than wheat bursting in the furrow, trod on,
Better than crowds driven back.
Better than a sea of tears hurling and swelling,
Your death protests with a shudder of the dawn
That rose over the still-bleeding Golgotha!

I listen, avidly, like the other Voice
Of the Divine Suicide on the Cross,
To these simple words of your last hope:
"I have wanted to die for a long time now,"
To regret the hour that you were born,

Your disgust for the flesh that you vanquished,
Your pale, vague glance over the earth,
Where nothing is conscious of its mystery,
Your pale regard turned back from the world
Where the filthy mob teems, blaspheming –
And turned back, thus, towards the other world,
        you said:
"I have wanted to die for a long time now."

There are no sweeter words than this,
In poems, fit for your tomb!
There is not, O Christ, God of sorrow, God supreme,
Among those who blaspheme you,
A single person who does not shudder at them.

Songs of the Journey

Songs of the Journey

I will be the queen of the palace, –
Will I be your queen if I please you?
But the prince passed by, without a regard.
She lifted her eyes towards the young wheat:
– I am the fiancée of Hazard! –

I will be the spouse of the house, –
Will I bake the bread of your harvest?
But the laborer turned away his regard.
He thinks about good weather for haymaking.
– I am the fiancée of Hazard! –

I will be the virgin of the altar, –
Will your gentle grace desire it?
And Christ on the cross, haggard, says:
Be the queen of the immortal Groom,
It is I, your fiancé, Hazard.

And I said to her:
"Do you imagine, sweet love, that your dream
Is sealed by a kiss merely?
That every song is fleeting?
That every promise is empty?
Do you imagine that your lips are sweet
For one quick second only?"
She said: "Your voice rebukes me
But your arm embraces me, my love!"

And I said to her:
"Do you know who I am? Who I was?
Who I will be, tomorrow, at matins?
Whether I am proud or confused
By your pink, childish pudor?
Do you know whether I merit the treasure
That I plunder from you in a fiery kiss?"
She said: "Are you not still
My father, my brother, and my God?"

And I said to her:
"Do you wish to die then,
Speaking to me in so distant a voice?
There is nothing more to say, o my Life,
No more human words!
And you? What are you to me, who embrace me
In a dream of Eternity?"
She said: "That thing that you fear most:
The death of your vanities!"

Everything that bleeds wine
From the presses of dawn's light
At the grey flank of amphoras, –
Will we drink it tomorrow?

And everything that rises in the West,
Clouds of lavished gold,
What tired gesture must
Amass it, this evening, for the lover's luxuries?

Spring, your thousands of emeralds, beautiful bright,
Will I tread on them, again, until another summer?
Our skies in solemn grayness, does a white winter
Wander over them since Eternity?

Believe: what does Life or Death matter,
In the ravishment of love?
Pray in your powerful soul:
What does night and day matter?
For you shall know vast dreams
If you know this one law:
There is no night beneath the stars,
And all darkness is within you.

Love: what does Shame or Glory matter,
To you whose turn it is?
Do you sing with a voice that carries
The message of all lovers?
For you will speak the song of splendors
If you tell your intimate emotion:
There are no fatal disasters,
Every defeat is within you.

Do not believe, – [3]
Because April laughed pink
In the orchard
Or grew pale with the voluptuous excess of flowers, –
That all things
Are according to our gay hearts,
And that there is no more thirst to quench.

Do not believe, –
Glorious in autumnal glories,
Drunk on gushed wines that the grain we tread on
          drinks of, –
That there is no more hunger that anything satiates:
For December is afoot in the pale night.

Yes, but do not believe, –
Because around you every soul is vile,
And the crowd adores its servile vice,
Because, on the plain where the Mystery pants,
Trampling on the corn spikes, crushing the leaf, with
          troubled wings,
The city grows, –

Do not believe, –
Though every heart is low, –
That the old Angelus forever sounds the death knell,
Believe, know, and shout it out loud
That Love is a conqueror and Hope is king!

---

[3]Editor's note: This stanza and what follows, to the end of this chapter, were added in a later edition of "Songs of the Journey." They are included here for completeness.

From a little sunshine and blonde sand
I fashioned some gold,
Whose ardent secret is not crouching
In the empty crucible of athanors:
It fell through my fingers with the sound
That gay flutes make;
It ran through my fingers
Into the water made moiré
By the windy games of Messidor.
From some dazzled wheat I fashioned snow
From old ages,

And from the wan smile of virginal girls
Who are wounded
By a word of joy strange in its promise,
A gesture
That goes dissipating in the procession
Of ephemeral dreams whose laughter lightens
The march of time, –
Until the threshold where love braids
The crimson symars of sacrilege:
I fashioned snow
From flower petals.

From the remaining hours of a hurried and bright life
I made eternity spiritual:
I took a pinch of salt in my hands
And cast it over the bitterness of the sea
According to the fate
Of frail and fragile things that one dreams eternal –
I took the salt
Of all our bittersweet tears
And I threw it into the face of death.

The whispered dream of graying leaves
Denounces with a laugh the least of breezes,
One feels it pass, wholly scented
By a little love, still! of some swooned flower...
The adolescent Year, with a left-handed gesture,
Rebraids, blushing, its loosened tresses,
Grows impatient, laughs, weeps, and grieves
In the diaphanous shade;

> *I hear Death scything,*
> *With Love tossing the wheat.*

She has awoken, all groggy from a dream:
April, the comely rider with the too fleeting song,
With one brutal kiss in passing has made her drunk,
So much so that, exhausted for all this long May, she
        lies in bed;
And awakens only at the sound of the sap...
Is it nostalgia for the previous evening? Is it a
        reproach?
She blushes, stretches, yawns, and sits up,
Half asleep, her soul undecided:
Is she absolved? Is she damned?
What drunken memory
And what hope presents itself?

> *I hear Death scything,*
> *With Love tossing the wheat.*

Dreamy, she gazes, sees, and is surprised by
A green darker than the monotonous forest,
A grass in full flower, so tall that it hides
The slow-moving river that junks ply;

The high, dusty hedge where vine branches grimp
Looks low, and the willows droop with their flowers;
The sun, inclined, turns the Hour pink with a kiss;
The tree trunks are ribboned by its rays.

> *I hear Death scything,*
> *With Love tossing the wheat.*

Now she listens, eyes half-closed,
To the flight of the agile air that grazes the water with
        a kiss
And bends towards her bosom a spike of wheat that
        grazes it;
She shivers and laughs for she has his word:
He will return, she says, and the hour is already near;
She watches intently, holding her breath, for his
        approach in the grass,
Treading on the sweet trefoil and bitter hemlock,
Serious, his smile like a shadow that glides...

> *I hear Death scything,*
> *With Love tossing the wheat.*

It's him! in his variegated June coat,
With all the flowers of the prairie inviolate,
Through the grass that he cuts down, the hedges that
        he leaps over,
Standing in silver stirrups, hand held high, it is the
Comely April rider at full gallop!
Prepare yourself with a welcoming smile to greet his
        lips;
It is the second kiss before the last mourning,
Before the inert summer that autumn profanes:

I hear Death scything,
With Love tossing the wheat.

He passes on, just as before, and the petals rain;
The rosebush, dispetaled, puts out new sepals;
It is the end of spring and young summer reigns;
The echo of some other April hymn he celebrated
Sounds, still, in his steps and flies from rock to vale!
His face is painted with May flowers and April
        laughter,
June is voluptuous and tired; the agile Hour
Mocks you and laughs at you, Ariadne's bright sister:

I hear Death scything,
With Love tossing the wheat.

The Ride of Yeldis

The Ride of Yeldis

The turrets that covered Her with their shadow
Rose like organ pipes against the sky,
Those evenings in June, with countless voices;
And, really, all the music
That vibrated on the terraces rich in honey,
Throughout that slow, sun-drenched June,
Was like one long canticle,
Of many voices, filled with wonder...

Yeldis welcomed us, from the windowsill,
Sometimes;
And sometimes we waited, with bated breath,
Seated on the porch, shaded in mourning,
To hear her singing like the springtime;
And the old man, her father or her spouse,
Held out a welcoming hand
To all those She lit up with a smile;
Those were the days of tears and laughter,
Serene evenings:
We came there like pilgrims...

The countryside was fertile and rich in wines,
Gay with the sun that is reflected in the sea
And the port
Was alive, morning and evening,
With the parti-colored crowd;
Every hour of the tide
Was filled with good hope,
Greetings, farewells:
Ships entered from every horizon,

From Carthage, Rome, and the East
And the North, and the mysterious West;
Vessels departed towards every horizon
– With their white sails, laughing almost...

Philarque and I, we kept an eye on the port;
And for wine, wheat, or for gold,
According to the exchange,
We took in amber or spices,
Emptying our cellars and granges
Depending on which way the winds blew.
That old man came to exchange strange gold,
One morning;
We knew his sort;
His gaze smiled, distant,
As if towards his long-dead youth,
He walked calmly in the tumult of the quays,
The shoutings, with the cries of the crow's nest on
            the lookout,
Toward the jetties;
And, as he told us his address
Outside the city, to the hill with the oak groves,
We went to bring him newer coins,
And we saw Yeldis among the flowers;
Philarque, counting the old gold ducats,
Thought he recognized her in the effigies
And had to count over, and messed up again...

We came there like pilgrims
Who devoutly go without thirst or famine:
Philarque and I and Luc and Martial –

The one grave, the other haughty –
And Claude with his little viol
Which (he said) consoles;
There were evenings of painful and sweet hours,
Sometimes. Yeldis singing, we all wept afterwards,
And we laughed at her clear laughter;
And on other evenings there were other words,
Some better, some worse...

One spring the old man died
– Just as people die, at daybreak –
As in a dream (it was said) uttering loving words
And blessing his life in death itself;
And when, in the cortege, She appeared,
In the full bloom of her rosy youth
And, despite some tears, replete with the aurora, –
Symbol of human joy:
Smiling although desolate –
It was like those funeral processions that go
From dawn to shadow, day to night,
Life to Death,
And April to winter, through the sunlit willow grove!

Philarque said to me, that evening, – alone, that
            evening –
Philarque said to me: "I love her," and I said to him:
"Philarque, we all love her," and saying that, I smiled;
And he gazed ahead, without seeing...
We knew that she was departing, that evening...

The porch was low, with its close

Grille of a triple-forged iron;
The terraces rose in tiers,
From fruits to flowers, to the arbors,
With the climbing vine and its muscles twisted
For the weight (it seemed) of gorged clusters...
Martial seized one of them, from the outside,
Brusquely, and saying in a half voice:
"We should be like this for Her,
And stop dispetaling her daisies
And swear to accept her choice,
Without quarreling."
– The sunset smiled pink from horizon to zenith –
We swore it over our immortal soul.

However
Yeldis with her train of sorrowful darkness
Came, in the rustling sound of the gravel under her
          feet,
Paler with her long eyes of amethyst
And her hair rose-colored and scaffolded;
Violet gloved, she... –
I see her, there,
As on that Chaldean eve,
Who said, from the other side of the grille, and – with
          a smile –
With a dismissive gesture: "Are you mad?

It is late; what did you come to tell me?"
We stayed there; but she, laughing again:
"The journey is distant," she said,
"From the edge of dawn,
And I go alone, without a knight even,
Without a squire who rides in the saddle!"
She laughed, as if to mock us,

Knowing that each one of us would follow her,
League after league, step after step,
Through false path and true path,
Until trespass.

Martial wanted to speak, but Luc the adroit,
          outmaneuvered him,
Before he could speak, and said, "I'm in!" –
"Me too!" said Claude; and, all of us, we said
          "Me!" –
Thus did it happen.

The sun was rising brightly when we set out;
The gay harnesses tinkled like rhymes...

Philarque was rich and of noble, antique stock,
Who came along the coasts of Africa,
With the Chaldean stars and all its arts,
To the West, via the exodus of the living;
He knew the secret of every hazard;
He had read the tomes of scholars;
He spoke of oases where the water is God-given;
He had strong words for beggars:
"Does the desert nourish the improvident?"
He said to them, chasing them away,
Then he laughed and gave them money;
He seemed old, sometimes, by a hundred years.

Luc was ruddy and a redhead:
He seemed an adolescent just out of childhood,
Despite being the oldest among us;

His father was from the cities of the Hanse,
His mother Venetian; he loved to drink;
He laughed, boisterously and vain, jealous to please;
I have seen him gay and sad in the same moment;
Prudent or reckless,
As the wind blows, and here is what he thought of
          life:
At times a poor disillusionment,
At times the scarecrow one defies.

Martial, Luc's mother's brother, was from Rome;
He was sweet to the ladies but unrequited,
He said so;
He walked alone among other men;
We were proud when we got to know him;
His life was a veil of sadness,
Old thoughts gray like the haze
Rattled around in him, who knows?
He was a master of souls grouped
Together by the action of his brain;
But he did not abuse his power:
He sang, as some people pray, very quietly and alone,
In the evening,
And slew with a glance, or with the sword;
His hatred was calm and inalterable
As was his one and only love.

Claude was pale, with a smile on his face,
Gay with a strange gaiety like a dream,
With a voice so soft in laughter
That it belied his raillery;
A gay lie
Veiled his soul with a certain effrontery,
Making dreams from his words;

He carried his viol over one shoulder
And played – playing –
Such bright tunes
With their sung imagery,
That mixed so well with the dreams of our heart,
That by the second refrain we had all joined in,
In a half voices, making up the choir;
He loved Yeldis with an astonishing love.

And when, Sun, in your lyrical Rays,
The cavalcade descended the hill
With bells tinkling and laughter,
I swear there was not a man alive who would not
      have sold
His heart, his soul, and his hope
To be one of us that evening...

We had some beautiful rides,
And tired but joyful stops:
Spurs to their flanks and bridles let loose,
Our horses, by dawn, entered into the day
And, from morning to night, passed at a gallop;
We made stops, tired or gay,
At the foot of a beech tree, on the verge of a suburb;
We arrived late and we left early.

One radiant day,
Philarque and Luc both quit the path
And rode off, without saying goodbye,
Towards the Western sun,
As if in flight;
Yeldis smiled and whipped her horse;

Martial and Claude turned away, pale;
And we followed her, the three of us, without saying
      a word.

That evening became stormy and dark;
At the top of a hill, we made a stop
Among the chestnut trees
Where we walked, treading on countless leaves;
The hour was grave and the darkness embraced me.
Yeldis spoke to us;
And, at night, starless and breathless,
Her voice alone existed, –
So it seemed to us –
And, despite her beautiful eyes, hair,
And svelte graces that during the day were revealed
For the beloved charm of her attire, –
A voice in the night, thus did she seem more beautiful
(One closes one's eyes to listen to music, right?
Thinking, one closes one's eyes to see more clearly,
      right?)

A person might think he was dreaming, listening to
      her:
She told us such things, such words,
That each grew in size like a dream, and sprouted
      wings,
And we did not dare believe everything, but we
      believed.

The past faded into the distance of yesterday
Without echo – like a vale of snow where winter
      sleeps; –

It opened out like a veil over our life;
The general darkness was brighter
Than the June sun at midday;
It was also like a smile;
The scents were different at night,
And her words were beautiful enough to die for.

I had followed her, from there, doubtless
For some futile and forgotten love of mine,
For that evening my soul was completely smitten
In a first stammered emotion;
This was not the awakening of a day after:
I no longer remembered the paths we had taken,
The bends, or the hours *en route*,
Of yesterday's span that fades into memory;
I loved her like Life itself and every joy,
Feeling myself born by her like a child
For some day, without end, whose morning hatches!

It was like a death whose eternity wells up,
The undreamt embrace of my obscure soul,
The sudden triumph of certitude,
The sudden blossoming, unexpected,
Of the chaste and pure flower
Which says within itself: everything is fine...

And we sobbed in the shadows, Elysians...
The wind started to blow, rhythming its phrases,
And when she fell silent, all the shade twittered,
And little by little, branch by branch,
The entire forest chanted as on a Sunday...

Since that evening then, since that night,

Which the phosphorescent shadow lit up,
Like the night through our eyelids,
Diffuse clarities, dull and bright;
Since that hour, I lived because of Her,
Since that glimmering night,
Effulgent with mystery...

At dawn we entered,
Four abreast, a town,
To the reveille of one hundred bugles,
To the confused cries of vile crowds;
Everything was topsy-turvy, and us and her,
And the hour and the dawn were supernatural;

Tall purple walls in perspective,
Leaned over us like river banks,
The towers, heavy and brutal, piled up vertically;
And, in the riverine sounds of the crowd
That stagnates and flows,
The clinking of irons,
The clear striking sound of iron horseshoes against
       the flagstones,
And, on the plaza, that river of people rolling and
       swelling,
Like a sea;
– And, always, the bugles in triumphant volleys,
And the brass and the iron.

Our horses trotted over dirty patriarchs
Whom a vow prostrated under our march.

Then, beneath the wide, low gate,
Armed men in array
Drew their sword and saluted us, three times;

As the flight of our gallop to the plain
Thundered over the drawbridge
Like a defiance,
And the sound of the human crowds
Died down suddenly,
Beyond the resurgent walls; –
We had returned to a spring in blossom.

Yeldis was regal,
And, as I was remembering the effigy
On the gold coins that Philarque had counted,
I saw her again, similarly and pale;
And I recalled the port and the crow's nest,
The quay, at day, at night, and each boat
And the old man who died without blaspheming;
She smiled more seriously and more distant.

The ride resumed;
The plains fell away behind us
With the sun and the day, sometimes the night;
The distant hills, which the dawn reveals,
Drew nearer on the slow, calm, and gentle evenings,
With the moon in the firmament and the stars
Twinkling through red branches;
Tall walnut trees lined the road, sometimes;
Passing under their shade we grew cold,
And we picked up the pace with a trot,
Without saying a word.

And Claude, one evening of rest, saying he was
        tired,
Looked at Yeldis and wanted to sing very softly;
He fell asleep – his head resting against her dress –
And he did not wake up again when dawn broke;
We buried him, Martial and me,
By a fountain that laughed like he did;
It was in the month
That one cuts the boxwood.

The plain opened up, immense, from then on;
The great repose of accomplished things
Meandered in a slow breeze through the wheat,
With the trembling of panoplies,
And sang softly, accompanied by church bells,
The harvest being near;
I felt that my soul was filled
With the calmness of the plain before harvest...

Martial, deathly pale (I can still see his face:
We had made a stop under a sycamore tree,
Near a silent stream that I drank from –
Kneeling on the ground and face to face
With my own reflection, – so close, that I was
        drinking
From between my own lips that were drinking –
And I stood up to listen to him:
His voice was steady with a certain audacity,
Trembling mildly as if he were afraid...)
Martial said – like someone reciting a poem:
"On my soul, I love you,
And I want to die, if it please you that I die;

But tell me the reason!..."
Yeldis, turning, smiled and drank
From the cup of water that she took from his hand,
Then, with a mocking gesture, she pointed out the
      road again. –
I see them still, there; without empty words,
The one pale and upright, the other enigmatic –
He walked towards her and took her hand,
Virile and frank;
She bowed her head like a child;
And, suddenly, beautiful in his full youth
And in his will and in his fine love
Without turning back,
He took her and, without a cry and without resistance,
Without a word spoken between them,
Jumped into the stirrups,
And giddyap! the horse reared and went into a
      gallop...

He was beautiful in his full youth,
She blushed for all his promises;
Doubtless their fates were bound.

The sun was setting and I watched their escape
Deeper into the crepuscule, in the direction of
      tomorrow;
And I remained standing in the road;
My heart beating more rapidly perhaps...
He was a good man and manly, and surely deserving
      of her.

So Philarque, who was a subtle scholar,

Took off to save his pride (is that what he thought?);
And Luc, handsome and smug, also took off,
To preserve a shadow of his vanity, without a care in
        the world;
Claude, who was always restless at heart,
Took off to sleep in the Lord;
Martial, who loves and desires, comely paladin,
Took off at a gallop, in the direction of tomorrow.

I am not ashamed of myself, thinking on it,
I have not the least regret for this poem:
I know that, for having followed Her
Under the chestnut trees, *I now know life*:

For me every shadow is bright, and the sun
Sings in the gold of the wheat and bees;
What I have from Her, She gave it to me;
Not a moment to ask forgiveness for;
With a single smile She made me thus;
If I had not been born for her kiss,
At the very least, I gave her my soul – She left
The secret of her soul to this heart of mine:
With one word She made an echo
That chants in the woods and murmurs over the
        water,
Which sounds and dies in the waves of the swell,
Which floats harmoniously in the cries of the crowd;
There is not a blade of grass that quivers,
There is not a pebble that rolls in the river,
Not a song in the autumn orchard,
Not a kiss on the spring path,
Not a drop of true blood in the West,
Not a sacred word vibrating in Poems,

That I do not weep over, or laugh over, that I do not
        love in Her.

ENVOI

Princess,
Since the break of dawn with its warm breath,
The harvesters have come towards the plain;
They have spoken many languages, in scattered
        groups,
Come from many lands, through many hazards;
I have joined them because, in autumn,
Every man is welcome who joins the harvest;
I followed them into the fields that day
And, bent over the sheaf that was gleaned for
        you,
I listen to the bells ringing in the evening,
And I think that Life is beautiful and full of Hope.

Other Books by the Publisher

Fanchette's Pretty Little Foot by Restif de La Bretonne

Je M'Accuse... by Léon Bloy

My Hospitals & My Prisons by Paul Verlaine

Salvation Through the Jews by Léon Bloy

Words of a Demolitions Contractor by Léon Bloy

Cellulely by Paul Verlaine

Ecclesiastical Laurels by Jacques Rochette de la Morlière

Flowers of Bitumen by Émile Goudeau

Songs for Her & Odes in Her Honor by Paul Verlaine

On Huysmans' Tomb by Léon Bloy

Ten Years a Bohemian by Émile Goudeau

The Soul of Napoleon by Léon Bloy

Blood of the Poor by Léon Bloy

Joan of Arc and Germany by Léon Bloy

A Platonic Love by Paul Alexis

The Revealer of the Globe: Christopher Columbus & His Future Beatification (Part One) by Léon Bloy